The Dragon and the Lemon Tree

Robert Walton

Robert Walton

Illustrations by Ginny Allen

Published by:

Pisces Press, Inc.
Rancho Santa Fe, California

Cover Design by David Aguero

ISBN 0-9623802-0-2
Library of Congress Number 89-092122

Dedication

This book is dedicated to Virginia Martin Walton. She was a fine teacher, a treasured friend to all who shared friendship with her, and a great lady. She was also my beloved mother. This book came too late for her to see this dedication, though she did read a first draft of the story. All of you who enjoy *The Dragon and the Lemon Tree* will honor her memory: she inspired a great deal of what I wrote.

R. M. Walton

Acknowledgments

I must give special thanks to John Norman, who greatly aided me in completing the final draft of this book. Also, I much appreciate the intelligent efforts of my proofreaders and critics—Phyllis Walton, Chris Meier, Ann Beckett, Jan Lombardi, Vicki McKean, Lincoln Hatch, Toni Ungs, and Jane Allen. Last of all, I wish to thank Gary Breschini for his indispensible expertise.

STORM

The sea's blue and silver back stretched to the edge of the sky. It lay quietly, rubbing against the land, sleeping in the sun. Towns, like barnacles on a great whale, clung here and there to its gleaming side.

One of these towns was often filled with the sound of bells, all sorts of bells. Bells on shop doors told of buyings and sellings. Bells on bicycles told of goings and comings. Bells in schools told of children captured and lessons begun. Bells on churches told of deaths and births.

But the oldest and largest bell of all was silent and had been silent for long years. It hung in a grim tower near the sea-wall. Its tone was the sound of midnight wind, for it was only rung when a great storm was known to be coming.

One day, shortly after noon, it began to ring. It rang three times and stopped. A moment went by. Three times, again, it rang and stopped. The people of the town stopped too. They listened, not quite believing what they had heard. Some looked at the sky and others, those who could, looked at the sea. Then the bell tolled again and all of the people began to move quickly.

In a small house near the harbor a mother spoke to her children, a boy and a girl. She said, "Hurry, get your coats."

The children slowly obeyed. They both looked worriedly at their mother. She was swiftly thrusting some of their clothes into a cloth bag. They then looked at each other in great puzzlement.

Mother spoke again, "It will be bad. They only ring the storm bell when it's going to be bad. It's been years since I've heard it. You two never have."

It hung in a grim tower near the sea-wall.

"Mother," the little girl said, "will our house be covered with water?"

Mother looked away and said, "I don't know, my darling. I don't know. That's why I'm taking you to the old man. He was a friend of my grandfather's. My grandfather used to take me to visit him when I was a small girl. He lives up on Starset, the hill west of town. There, at least, you'll be safe from the sea. Your father and I will stay here and fight the storm."

The children sat in silence, staring at her, their eyes large and shining. She looked back at them and said, "Come, I must be back before dark."

The children looked around the room. Their eyes were filled with the warm shadows of things they knew — the brown chair, the table, the yellow lamp. Mother touched their heads, rubbed their necks softly and said, "We must go."

They walked swiftly through the town. The children looked from side to side, for much was going on. Men were hammering boards over windows. Thumps and bangs echoed between old walls as wagons were hastily loaded. Many people were moving toward the landward gate. Men's eyes reflected gray sky. The hands of small children were being held by someone older and in the hard voices of old women they could hear storm winds coming.

Past the gate, mother took them on a steep path which led across fields and into forest. The daytime darkness of tall trees soon rested over them. Silence was cool and damp beneath their feet. The noise of the town was left far behind. They climbed.

Just as both of the children were about to complain, the path left the trees. They were tired, but there was something new to see. The brow of the hill lay before them. Mother didn't stop.

Clouds raced over them. Rags of mist streamed through tree-tops behind them.

Ahead was a low house made of logs. Surrounded by tall grass and with grass growing on its sod roof, it seemed more like a burrow than a house. Two small windows, heavy with hidden purpose like half-closed eyes, stared out at them. Both children shivered. Mother walked straight up to the stout wooden door and knocked.

A voice as dry as old leaves said, "Come in."

They did. They found themselves in a warm, dark room. The coals of a large fire glimmered in a hearth made of mudbricks. A black pot hung from an iron hook above the hearth. The children could hear a bubbling sound coming from the pot.

An old man stood near it with a wooden spoon in his hand. He was bald and his back was bent like a Christmas bow. His ears stood out from his head like two sails. His eyes glowed like stray embers from the fire.

He said, "It's been winters and springs since I've seen you, girl . . . you and your grandfather."

The children now saw something strange. Their mother lowered her eyes. Years fell away from her. She suddenly seemed to be no older than they. Red-faced, she stared at her toes and said nothing.

The old man spoke again, "It doesn't matter, girl. It doesn't matter. Your grandfather has been dead for twelve years now and I am cranky — best left alone. My time is storm time. It comes now, eh? I feel it. The world is due for a shaking."

Mother said, "Yes, the town is all astir. Walls must be braced. Bags must be filled with sand. I have to help. I've brought my children to you."

"I see," said the old man.

Mother, still unsure of herself, stammered, "Will . . . will you take care of them?"

"Of course," said the old man. He chuckled, "Of course, just as I once took care of you. Now, go back to your husband. You both have much to do. Your children will be safe, safer than you will be. Go. And God be with you."

Mother smiled . . . and suddenly grew older again. Quickly she stooped and kissed both of the children. She then turned, walked to the door, opened it and disappeared into a strange noontime gloom.

The children turned their stricken eyes from the door and found that the old man was looking at them. He smiled a toothless smile. They looked back at him and did not smile at all. He said, "Do you have toys?"

They nodded.

"Good," he said, "play with them. I have my work to do. Stay out of my way and everything will be fine." He turned away. The children looked at each other.

They looked back at him and did not smile at all.

All that long afternoon they stayed out of his way. All that long afternoon the wind's voice grew louder. Night was near when its moan pulled their eyes to the window. Cold and wild darkness poured in at them through the glass. Fear kindled in them with small flames of ice.

The old man said, "Come to the table. Supper is ready." They turned and their fear was gone. He gave them thick soup, brown, crusty bread, and mugs of bitter beer. They ate and were filled with food's good warmth.

When they were finished, the old man said, "We must wash the dishes. I could tell you a story while we work. Would you like that?"

The children looked at his glowing eyes and then at each other. They did not wish to irritate this very strange old man. Silently, they agreed to listen and, almost at the same instant, they nodded yes.

The old man laughed out loud, "Good, good. Ah, children, you do amuse me. Perhaps I can amuse you as well."

The children, their faces as still as a pond on a summer eve, watched the old man carefully. He regarded them for a moment and then thrust his head forward, "Do you have confidence? Do you believe in yourselves?"

Mystified and more than a little alarmed, they shook their heads and drew back.

"I thought not. My story will be of some value to you then. Also," he nodded slyly, "it has a dragon in it."

The boy, interested in spite of himself, said, "A dragon? A real dragon?"

"Yes! It has a dragon in it and talking beasts, and magic — magic of a special sort." The old man paused.

Outside, the storm began to rage. Drops of rain shattered against the logs of the house. Wind fell on the mountain's crown like a bear's heavy paw. Nothing moved or lived in the open.

The old man handed each of the children a rough towel. He then plunged his hands into a bowl of warm, soapy water and said, "Once there was an orphan boy named Thomas. He was terribly poor and he had no home. He was not a bad boy, but his life was not a happy one. On a morning just before winter . . . ."

SEA JOURNEY

Thomas kicked a rock. It skittered over rough paving stones. He kicked it again and it bounced off of a wall with a satisfying smack. A red face appeared in a window near. Angry words bit at his heels as he rounded a corner. He ran until he could run no more.

The fishermen's square was before him. Beyond it was gray water. He walked to the edge of the seawall and stopped. He looked idly at some fat gulls sleeping on pilings. He then looked down and saw a sturdy boat. Its bow was covered over and its timbers were heavy, strong. It was made for poking its head into great sea waves. A rope led from its stern to an iron ring set in the stone by his feet.

Thomas looked quickly around. No one was paying any attention to him. In two hops he was down the stairs and sitting on one of the boat's rough benches.

A chill wind blew down around the pilings, ruffled the gulls' feathers. Thomas shivered. His coat was thin and worn. He shivered and almost rose to leave. He didn't because he was at last safely alone and he wanted to stay that way.

Not much good had happened to him that day. Rain falling on his eyelids had awakened him. The fat baker had then caught him trying to steal a roll. He looked at his bruised knuckles and wished that he'd been able to hold onto it. His empty stomach felt like a larger bruise.

He scratched his knee uneasily and looked at the restless waters of the harbor. He wished, not for the first time, that some kind stranger would walk up and offer to buy him a dish of soup and some warm bread. The wind poked its cold fox's nose up his sleeve. He shivered again.

"Get out of my boat!" said a voice. Thomas nearly fell into the water with surprise. "Get out, I say. Out!" The voice was loud and as jagged as a broken fingernail. Thomas looked up.

There was no friendliness in the face he saw. Small, hard eyes stared into his. A fisherman's beard, all spikes and wire, ran down a long jaw. The nose was a knife's blade. The mouth was a hook. It opened and the harsh voice again sounded, "I'm going to beat the tar out of you, thief!"

Thomas moved without thinking. In one motion he slipped the rope off its cleat and pushed against a stone piling. The boat's stern swayed away from the dock. The fisherman was down the steps in a heartbeat. He gathered himself on the last step and leaped.

Unfortunately, his right foot slid in dark grease. Face first, he soared into the sky. His arms made flying motions, but slowly he came down anyway. He landed with a smack in the harbor's cold water.

The fisherman came thrashing to the surface. He was angrier than a wet lion. He roared and then choked as a wavelet filled his mouth with bitter salt water. Thomas understood his danger. He swiftly shipped the boat's oars and began to row.

There was only one direction in which he could go — toward the sea. He hoped to come back in later at a different place. He could then abandon the boat and slip back into town. It was not to be.

The ebb-tide took him. Faster, faster he went away from land. He stopped rowing, for he was no fool. He knew that he couldn't fight the tide and hope to win.

He pulled the oars inside and looked around. Long, gray waves rolled up to his boat, lifted it high, and passed on toward land. Each one seemed to stare coldly at him before it dove beneath his feet. He shivered.

He saw a locker in the bow of the boat. He crawled to it and opened it. Inside, he found a warm jacket, oilskins, a bottle of water, some hard biscuit and a rope. He put on the jacket. He thought for a moment and then struggled into the waterproof clothes. Everything was far too large for him, but he felt much warmer than he had before.

Thoughtfully, he took a small drink of water. He screwed the cap down tight and put the bottle back in the locker. He put the biscuit next to the bottle. He would need it more later. He closed the locker and fastened it well.

The rope still lay beside him. He looked at the sky. Clouds grew fingers of wind and made darkness out of air. A storm was nearly upon him. He tied the rope around himself with a double knot, looped it around the sturdy seat and knotted it again. There was then nothing for him to do but be afraid. And soon he was.

The waves became larger, rougher. Water came into the boat. He threw it out with a small bucket. His back began to hurt from the pounding of the seat. Spray stung his eyes. Night came. Darkness swept over him like one of the storm's waves, a wave greater and blacker than its brothers.

Thomas fought the sea. He scooped up water with the small bucket and poured it overside. His arms began to ache from the bailing, but always there was more water. Then the cold seemed to go right through his clothes and his arms would move no more. That cold cut into him like a knife of ice. Somewhere between pain and cold and darkness, he lost his fear. He lay down beneath the boat's seat and waited for whatever might happen.

Morning came. Cold and lonely, it stole over the ocean's gray waters. Land was nowhere to be seen, but the storm had eased a bit.

Thomas drank a little water and chewed on half of the biscuit. He watched waves and hoped that the wind would push him back to shore. Hours filled with wind and emptiness rolled past him.

Night returned. Darkness opened high above him.

Stars shone dimly through spray and flags of cloud. The waves were far smaller, all their storm strength gone. Cold and weary past thinking, Thomas sat watching the stars, waiting for the end of their long dance.

Morning came again. The sun rose swiftly and Thomas stretched in its warmth. Orange light filled the clear sky. The sea had settled into long, smooth, rolling waves. The boy fell asleep even before he decided that was what he wanted most to do.

He awoke at midday. The sun was white and far above him. Warm, blue air lay over him like a blanket. He sat up. In every direction only midnight blue water could be seen. But the ocean seemed nearly friendly now. Waves slid gently beneath the tiny boat.

Thomas crawled forward to the locker. He opened it and got out his water bottle. He took a drink, a small one. More than half of his water was gone. He screwed the cap on tightly and put the bottle away. With some disgust he reached for the last of the biscuit. It was hard and chalky. He nibbled at it and thought. An idea flashed into his mind.

He again reached into the locker. He felt around for several moments. There! Carefully, he pulled out a length of fishing line. Attached to it were three hooks and a lead weight.

Raw fish is not nearly so unpleasant as you might suppose. Many people choose to eat it that way and like it very well. To Thomas it seemed at least as good as stale biscuit. In fact his mouth watered as if a fish had already been hooked, pulled in and lay wriggling in the bottom of the boat.

With great care he untangled the line. He removed two of the hooks and put them in his pocket. After all, he might catch too big a fish on his first try. He would need the other hooks if he lost the first one.

He looked at the one hook and thought. After a moment, he carefully tore a small square of white cloth from his undershirt. He put this on the hook. It was poor bait, but it would have to do.

He lowered the baited hook into the water. Several minutes passed. He sighed and jiggled the line. Several more minutes passed. He paid out line until only a few feet lay on the seat beside him. Slow, lazy waves lifted the boat toward the sun.

Suddenly, there was a tremendous jerk on the line. Thomas was nearly pulled over the side of the boat. He had wrapped a turn of line around his hand. Only this saved him from losing his fishing gear.

After the one great pull, there was nothing. He looked distrustfully down into clear water. He could see only the faraway darkness of unlighted deeps. Hand over hand, he pulled his line back in. To his great surprise he found that his bait was gone and that his hook was now as straight as a pin.

At that moment a squeaky sort of voice sounded

behind him, "You are very rude!"

Thomas jumped to the other side of the boat. This set it to rocking violently. It took several seconds for him to steady it. When he was at last able to peer over the gunwale, he found himself staring into the cool, dark eye of a porpoise.

It spoke again, "I said that you are very rude. None of your kind has ever been here before. I expected none of your barbs, especially so deep. You've managed to cut me quite painfully."

Thomas gasped, "You . . . you can talk!"

The porpoise looked at him silently for a moment. Then it said, "Of course I can — when I have something which needs to be said. You have seriously disrupted my day."

Thomas blinked. He then noticed a long red line which curved down the porpoise's side. He said, "I didn't mean to hurt you. I was just trying to catch a fish."

The porpoise said, "Whether you meant to or not, you have hurt me. I *am* hurt. I expect an apology, though it embarrasses me to have to tell you so."

Thomas turned red. He chewed on his lip and became sulky. The porpoise snorted, looked disgustedly at him and turned to leave. Only the smallest pang of guilt, mixed with loneliness and good sense, saved him at the last second from great foolishness. He shouted, "Wait! Wait! I do apologize! I am sorry that I hurt you.

I'm lost. I have no food. I wanted to catch a fish, not you."

The porpoise turned again and flashed back to the side of the boat. It lay still in the water looking mildly at Thomas. At last it said, "I accept your apology. Also, I guessed rightly about your present situation. Could you use my help?"

Thomas lowered his eyes and said, "Yes, I can use anyone's help now, even yours."

The porpoise snorted again and said, "You really do have no manners! My help will be far more than you expect it to be. Still, if it were no more than a kind word, you should be thankful for it."

Thomas studied his shoes and said nothing.

The porpoise said, "I will return. Do not try to catch any fish while I am away. Please!"

Thomas looked up and was about to speak. The porpoise was gone. He sighed and leaned back against the seat. He hadn't caught a fish, but he had managed to offend the porpoise. It would very likely not return. He sighed again and, suddenly drowsy, began to doze. An hour filled with warm sunshine passed.

Then the boat hit something with a solid thump. Thomas sat up. There was another bump which no wave could have caused. He looked over the rail right into the great, somber eye of a whale. He jumped back so quickly that he banged his elbow hard on the seat. There was a whistling sound from the other side of the boat.

"I told you I would bring a large amount of help!" It was the porpoise. There was again a whistling sound. Thomas knew it to be laughter. He was still too shaken to be able to see the joke.

The porpoise went on, "My friend here will push or pull you to a place where your kind lives. It's not too far by our reckoning, but it would be easier for her to pull you than to push you. Do you have a . . . a . . . ? It's very long. It's like the thinnest part of a tall seal-tree. Have you one of those?"

Thomas could hardly think. For several moments he was silent. The answer finally came to him. He said, "You mean a rope. Yes, I have a rope!" He scrambled forward to the locker. He had coiled the rope and put it away after the storm. Quickly he pulled it out and held it up.

The porpoise said, "Yes, we need one of those. A rope, a rope — I must remember that. Now fasten one end of it to your boat. Give the other end to me."

Thomas tied the rope around his boat's foremost cleat. He placed the other end in the porpoise's open mouth and said, "How will you tie it to the whale? You have no hands."

The porpoise looked at him for a long moment, snorted again, and dove beneath the water. The whale moved slowly up to the bow of the boat. The great eye gazed at him as its owner glided past. Somehow, Thomas knew that the whale was amused.

He could not see how it was done, but the rope was attached to the whale's mouth. In an instant he felt the boat begin to move. It was magical — the quick slap of small waves on the bow, the cool breeze against his face, the sea's vast peace.

The porpoise sported alongside. Thomas would have liked to talk with it, but that was impossible. The smooth motion continued. Hours went by. Thomas lapsed into a sort of daze.

Suddenly, he sat up. Something had changed. The boat was no longer moving. He looked carefully over the bow. In front of him, across a small stretch of sea, mountains rose steeply into the sky.

The porpoise whistled for his attention. Thomas turned. It said, "Well, here you are. Needless to say, I don't know much about what is up there. I do know that there are others like you living somewhere near. I'm sure you can find them. Good luck!"

Thomas called out, "Thank you! Thank you! You saved my life!"

The porpoise rolled on its side, "Don't mention it. Just remember not to put any fishhooks in the deep waters near here. That's all the thanks I ask!"

Thomas said, "I won't. And please thank the whale for me!"

"Thank her yourself!" shouted the porpoise as it turned and disappeared into the silver-blue crest of a wave.

Thomas felt the boat rise as if it were on a large wave. He looked down. The whale was within a yard of his hand. Her calm eye once more looked mildly upon him. Thomas shouted, "Thank you and good-bye!"

She slid smoothly by. A few yards away, she dove. Her tail came out of the water, rose high in the air, paused and came slapping down like a giant's hand. There was an explosive clap and a great, silver fan of spray opened wide in the air above Thomas. He laughed as the cool droplets splashed over him. The whale had said good-bye to him in her own special way. He watched her swim into blue distance.

There was a bump. He turned and found the tide had nudged his boat onto a sandbar. It would carry him all the way to shore if he could get his boat off the sand. He hopped over the side into ankle deep water. The sea was pleasantly cool on his feet and legs. He pushed and the boat floated free. He pushed it again and it floated to the edge of the bar. He stepped hastily back in.

The boat's blunt bow was soon nosing gently against a sandy beach. Thomas again hopped out. He looked around and quickly found something he needed, a large driftwood log. He took the rope which was still attached to the bow and wrapped its other end around the log. He tied a good knot in the rope, just in case. He hoped that he wouldn't have to ride in the boat again, but he couldn't be sure about that. After all, the island might be home to head-hunters or cannibals.

Thomas walked down the beach. He came to a stream which disappeared into damp sand at the edge of the sea. He followed it back up toward the island's heart and soon found grass beneath his feet. The stream now bubbled over round stones and slipped suddenly into deep places. He knelt beside a clear pool and drank. The water was sweet, cold. It washed away the dry salt of the sea and filled him with its gentle strength. He drank until he could hold no more.

Breeze rustled tree leaves near. He sat back and thought. What could he do? Which way should he go? The leaves continued whispering but spoke no answers to his questions. He shrugged and rose. There could be no answers to such questions. He could only follow the stream and hope for the best. He set out.

The stream led him a weary way up and up into steep hills. An hour passed and then another. His mind began to wander. He hardly noticed where his feet were taking him. He felt as if he had been climbing forever.

He suddenly became aware that the patterns of colors before his eyes had changed. He stopped. He was no longer in the midst of sunlit forest. He was in what looked like a garden. A garden?

He heard voices. He turned quickly and saw their owners. Two strange looking people were standing still, watching him.

Two strange looking people were watching him.

FIRST NIGHT

The old man's eyes were shining. He was silent for long moments. The children became impatient. The girl finally said, "What happened next?"

The old man looked at her, "Not now. Our dishes have long been done. And the storm will last through tomorrow."

The boy said, "Oh, please! We won't be able to sleep if we don't know what happened next."

The old man said nothing. His bright eyes rested on the children. His was a heavy gaze and the weight of it forced their eyes down. They began to feel most uncomfortable. Finally, he said, "It is time for bed."

The children did not argue further. The old man showed them to a dark corner of the cabin. A large bunkbed filled most of the corner. They took off their shoes and clambered up its rough sides. The boy took the bottom bed and the girl took the top one. They quickly snuggled down among soft, heavy quilts. The old man, his back to the fire, watched them.

Remembering to be polite, the children at last mumbled a good-night. The old man simply nodded. The few hairs on his head flashed silver-gold in the glow of the flames. He turned and went back to his hard chair.

The children lay still under their covers. Their

minds full of whales and silvery sunlight, the storm's roar did not bother them. Soon, they slept.

****

Morning came, gray and cold. The children rubbed sleep from their eyes with icy water. Breakfast awaited them on the table — toasted bread, thick plum jam, buttery fried eggs. They ate heartily while the old man sipped clear tea. Wind whined around the cabin's walls.

Breakfast over and dishes done, the children played in front of the fire. They wanted very much to hear the end of the old man's story, but he didn't seem to want to tell it. He was busy at a large desk near the door, carving a dark piece of wood. From muttered grumbles and disgusted snorts, they gathered that his work was not going well. Time passed.

Just before noon they fed the three red hens — Mathilda, Princess and Sam. They had been fluttering and clucking nervously, but they calmed down quickly at the soothing sound of the old man's voice. Perky, the rooster, strutted up and pecked at the old man's hand, just to let him know who was in charge. The old man laughed and then turned to the children. "Let's eat," he said.

They lunched on smoked fish, bread, onions and tea. They again cleaned the dishes and went back to their warm places before the fire.

But there were sounds outside. In the twilight of

the afternoon, a great, hungry storm-bear walked. The children heard its breathings. They shivered and stopped their play.

The old man pulled his chair over to them. He sat down and said, "I'll continue my story . . . if you like." The children sat forward. The old man began . . . .

I'm no giant. I'm a boy.

A GARDEN AND NEW FRIENDS

Thomas squinted his eyes against bright sunlight. The two figures were a woman and a man. Both were holding hoes. Both wore wide yellow hats and green work clothes. Thomas decided that they didn't look like head-hunters. Their garden was well kept. He saw fat tomatoes and ripe strawberries. A tiny ripple of hope, like the first touch of breeze on a still pond, ran through him.

The woman and the man came toward him. He opened his eyes as wide as he could and was surprised. They were tiny, a foot or more shorter than he was.

The woman said, "Who are you, giant? Where did you come from?"

Thomas blinked, "I . . . I'm no giant. I'm a boy."

The woman smiled, "Well, you look like a giant to me. What do you want in our garden? Are you hungry?"

Thomas said, "I was following the stream and found myself here. Yes, I am very hungry. Have you some food to spare?"

The man and the woman looked at each other. The man then looked back at Thomas and said, "Yes. Come along home with us. First, though, tell us your name."

"My name is Thomas. Who are you?"

The woman said, "I'm Columbine and this is my husband, Pepper."

Thomas, remembering the porpoise, tried hard to use his best manners. He bowed and said, "Pleased to meet you."

Pepper laughed and said, "The pleasure is mutual, I'm sure. Now, Thomas, you can earn your supper. Carry that basket for us, please."

Thomas quickly walked to where the little man pointed. He found a basket filled with brightly colored fruits and vegetables. He bent and lifted it to his shoulder. The man motioned for him to follow.

They walked between even rows of plants. They reached a hedge with a gate in it. Thomas shifted his hold on the basket and walked through the gate. He found himself on a narrow path a little above the stream.

Suddenly, he heard a high-pitched lowing sound behind him. He turned. Six golden cows were following him along the path, but they were no larger than large dogs. He couldn't help standing, staring.

Pepper said, "What's the matter? You do have cows in your country, don't you?"

Thomas said, "Yes, of course, but they are bigger, much bigger!"

Pepper looked at him thoughtfully, "Yours must be a strange and dangerous land indeed. You shall have to tell us about it. First, though, we have a great deal to do before sundown. Come." He turned and began to walk up the path.

Thomas followed again but paid much closer attention to his surroundings than he had before. He saw interesting things. There were bright blue birds the size of grasshoppers and a gray rabbit the size of a mouse. Butterflies floated like colored snowflakes above tiny flowers.

The path became steeper. Thomas began to feel weak. The sun was hot on his head and sweat dripped from the end of his nose. He watched the plodding of his own feet on the stony path.

A cool breeze brushed hair from his eyes. He looked up. A house made of rough logs stood above the trail and across the stream. A bridge led to its door. Flower boxes filled with blue and yellow blossoms hung below each of its windows. A small brook ran through a stone tunnel beneath its bottom floor and joined the large stream beneath the bridge.

Columbine was already halfway across the bridge and Pepper was close behind her. Thomas hurried up the path. He reached the bridge and took four quick steps out onto its old planks. There was a fearsome creaking sound. He stopped, frightened.

Pepper turned and saw Thomas's white face. He

laughed, "Come on, Thomas. Our bridge is sound. It always makes noises like that."

Thomas looked doubtfully at the gray boards. He stepped slowly over the length of the bridge, ignoring its groaning as much as he could.

He walked up to the green front door. He lowered the basket and, smiling as he did so, ducked his head as he went through it.

He walked up to the green front door.

He found himself in a dark, wide room. Its ceiling was two feet above his head. That was a relief! A long table and many chairs, richly carved, stood against the far wall. A large fireplace took up much of the wall to his left. He could see an iron stove nested among its stones. On his right was a small waterfall. The brook came right through the house.

Columbine said, "Thomas, put the basket over there. Pepper and I will soon have dinner ready. Drink some cool water if you wish."

He did so wish. First he put the basket on a wooden counter which was attached to the fireplace. Then he walked over to the brook. He knelt down and found a long-handled cup hanging from an iron hook. He dipped it into the swiftly flowing water, raised it to his lips and drank deeply.

Columbine and Pepper were both busy at the wooden counter. Choppings and mixings and stirrings were rapidly taking place. The fire had been stoked and was glowing redly. Thomas sighed and lay back on a wooly rug. Hidden bells of falling water rang softly in his ears. He slept.

"Thomas! Thomas! Supper is ready." Pepper turned and walked back to the large table against the wall. Thomas raised himself off of the rug and shook his head. Threads of sleep still fluttered across his eyes.

He looked up and found a happy sight. A dozen tall candles shone brightly along the length of the table.

Steaming dishes of food had been set on its smooth, brown surface. Pepper said, "Come, Thomas, we've set you a place. Sit on this bench here. You are rather too large for any of our chairs."

Thomas seated himself just as Columbine came up carrying a pitcher of cold milk. She said, "We've fixed a large supper. We expect that giants eat quite a lot." Thomas smiled and did not disagree.

Long moments of serious eating followed. The food was good and plentiful: a mixed grill of tomatoes, onions, mushrooms and bacon topped with toasted cheese; dark bread spread thickly with pale butter; spiced apples baked with raisins and sugar; new potatoes

He looked up and found a happy sight.

perfectly boiled and sprinkled with parsley. Thomas felt himself becoming more comfortable than he had been in a very long time.

When supper was over, he helped Columbine clear things off of the table. Pepper rolled up his sleeves and readied the dishwater. Soon dishes were done and dried. Thomas, eager to help his new friends, put things away on the top shelves of a cupboard. This was no trouble for him, for he could easily touch the ceiling of the house.

Pepper rubbed his hands on a rough towel and said, "Well, done is done! Let's sit in front of the fire. A glass of blackberry wine would go nicely now. Also, it's time we heard your story."

They moved over to the hearth. Columbine and Pepper sank into deep, soft chairs. Thomas sat on the floor and leaned on a pile of pillows. He sipped from a glass Columbine had given him. The wine was dark and clear. It tasted both fiery and sweet at the same time.

Columbine said, "Now, Thomas, how did you come to our small island? Only once in a hundred years does a stranger, a giant like you, come to our shores. Your journey must have been a long one!"

Thomas smiled and said, "It was." He went on to tell them his story and a good deal more. He told of the storm-dark sea. He told them of the friendly porpoise, of the great whale. He told of bald shopkeepers with squinty eyes and cruel hands. He told of dull, brown hours in school. He told of his lost family, his dead grandfather, his long and lonely wanderings. He told of sleeping cold and afraid in deserted barns and black forests. All of his needs and pains — many he could not name — peered like ghostly faces out around his words at Columbine and Pepper. Their lumpy lonely features saddened that kindly pair. Finally, Thomas was done.

Pepper leaned forward, "A proper nasty place you make your country sound, Thomas! Orphans find good homes, willing friends quickly in this island! We'll have no chilly sleeping tonight! You shall sleep here, before the fire. Several rugs thrown down should make it soft enough. Tomorrow, we'll put you to work. There is much to be done on a farm. We must go to market at week's end. Now, to sleep with us all."

After much bustling and some rolling, Thomas was comfortable. He murmured his good-nights as Pepper and Columbine climbed the stairs to their room. The fire burned low. He slept. Shadows grew long and old on the beams of the ceiling.

LATE AFTERNOON

"Hold for a moment," said the old man. "I'll continue in a bit, but I must have a sip of beer first. I always do at this time in the afternoon, storm or no." He arose and walked to a shelf near the sink. He took down a large pewter mug and turned to the beer keg near the wall. The children watched as he filled the mug with dark, frothy beer. He turned to where they sat, settled himself, and took a long, rather noisy drink from the mug.

The girl, holding back a smile, said, "What did you mean yesterday when you spoke of confidence? What does that have to do with Thomas?"

The old man looked up from his beer, "Ah, don't you see? Thomas has none, confidence that is. He drifts. He is afraid."

"But," said the boy, "so many bad things happened to him. How could he be otherwise?"

The old man sipped noisily again and looked at him. Then he grinned and nodded toward the window, "There are always storms, boy, always. There is fear; there is loss; there is danger. No human life is entirely free of them. There are shadows, near or far, in every future, every past." The old man paused and looked down into the brown depths of his mug, "But must a person be driven by these things?"

The girl frowned slightly in puzzlement at the old man's musings. Her young mind — a butterfly with sunlight on its wings — then flew lightly on. She said, "Well, what about the dragon? When will it come?"

"Yes," said the boy, "and the magic. What about that?"

The old man licked a speck of foam off of his upper lip and looked at them steadily. At last he said, "You want dragons and magic, eh? Well, listen . . ."

OF MAYORS AND DRAGONS

Thomas smiled with delight and surprise. They had risen before the sun that morning and had eaten a hurried breakfast. They had led ten tiny burros loaded with baskets of produce over misty mountain trails. They now stood together on the last ridge above the town called Silvershell.

New sunlight struck gold from amber roofs far below. Two arms of land spread out from either side of the town to nearly encircle a deep harbor. White fishing boats floated like sleeping gulls on its calm surface.

Pepper said, "It's a good town, the only one on this island. You will like its people, I think. The mayor is a windy sort, but kindly as such people go."

Columbine laughed and said, "Yes, Thomas, he puffs mightily, but be polite to him. He may be able to give you some help in getting back to your own country."

Thomas looked at her and looked quickly down again. The thought of leaving his friends and their beautiful island had not entered his mind. It was a disturbing thought. He had felt both happy and safe for nearly a week. He did not want this time of happiness to end so soon.

Pepper watched him and nodded wisely, "You know, Thomas, we've not spoken yet of your future. Getting back to your country will not be easy. You may not want to try at all. Anyway, you don't have to decide now. You are welcome to stay with Columbine and me for as long as you like. You are strong. We'll find more good work for your hands. Besides, it seems that you like our cooking!"

Thomas smiled gratefully and looked up. The small man's eyes were twinkling.

Columbine said, "Come, you two. We're late. We'll miss the market entirely!" They set off again down the steep trail.

The market turned out to be a large, flat area paved with gray stones. It was right next to the harbor. People who had things to sell sat on brightly colored rugs and did their business in the morning sun.

Thomas stood by a noisy fountain while Pepper and Columbine began to unload the burros. He watched several hundred very small people buying, selling, trading the day's news and just visiting.

Then silence swept over the crowd like a wind. The people of Silvershell had noticed Thomas and words just born died on their lips. Many hundreds of wide eyes turned toward him. He began to feel more than a little embarrassed.

Pepper spoke out of the side of his mouth, "I was afraid something like this might happen. You are so very large, Thomas. We may have to make some sort of speech or something."

Columbine leaned close, "Wait, here comes the Mayor. He will surely say everything that needs to be said . . . and more."

Across the plaza came a fat little man with a shiny bald head. His coat was of the softest red velvet. His breeches were royal blue. The brass buckles of his shoes darted fiery spears of light back at the sun. Threads of silver and gold gleamed from his vest. A medallion of heavy gold hung from a chain around his neck. Like the proudest and most important of all roosters, he strutted slowly up to where they were standing.  He stopped, put his hands firmly on his hips and said, "Who, large sir, are you?"

Thomas glanced around. All eyes were still on him. He took a deep breath, opened his mouth and . . . nothing came out. His voice seemed to be frozen. He had a desperate desire to run and hide.

Pepper came to his rescue, "Mayor Wiggin,

honored servant of the public weal and esteemed friend, it gives me great, great pleasure to introduce you to this shipwrecked traveler from a far land." Pepper faced Thomas and winked broadly. "He is a most important personage in his own country. The sea dealt him a cruel blow. His great ship was cast up on our island. He came upon my wife and me as we worked in our garden. Much had he suffered in the wilds above the western shores. We offered him the comfort of our home. Now, we have brought him to Silvershell, the center of our island civilization."

The mayor eyed first Pepper and then Thomas. He puffed up his chest and said, "Quite so. Quite so. Ehhhh . . . what is your name?"

Thomas thought quickly. The mayor reminded him very much of a principal he had once known. He suddenly felt at ease once again. In his very best before the principal manners he answered, "My name is Thomas, sir. And I am very honored to meet you." He bowed as gracefully as he could.

The mayor said, "Hah! Quite so. We were at first startled by your . . . by your . . . gigantic size. We are unaccustomed to having visitors from the lands of the giants."

Thomas bowed again, "I'm very sorry if I surprised you."

The mayor gazed out over the crowd with a gleam in his eye, "Think nothing of it, my boy. Think nothing of it. You are, of course, welcome to our fair city. We will assist you in any way that we can. In fact, speaking for the citizens here gathered, I must say that we are proud, proud to have a guest of you stature among us!"

The mayor was interrupted at this point by loud cheers and much clapping. The people of Silvershell knew their mayor well. They were not about to give him a chance to make a lengthy speech. The mayor looked somewhat disgruntled. Pepper grinned openly . Thomas smiled politely.

At that instant a shadow fell over the market place. All eyes turned upwards in search of the hidden sun. Thomas looked upwards too. His mouth fell open with disbelief at what he saw.

Hovering high above was a monstrous animal. It had a long, scaly body, four stumpy legs ending in glistening claws, two great bat's wings, a flat snaky head, and jaws full of ivory daggers. Everyone was too shocked to move or speak. The winged beast seemed to be pinned against the sky.

Then a skinny boy close to Thomas shouted, "It's a dragon!"

The dragon, for a dragon it was, heard the boy's shout and swung its body around. Some people ran and some fell to the ground, while others stood still and watched to see what would happen next. The dragon tilted its wings forward and dove. Low it swooped, roaring like an avalanche of stones. A blast of red flame

It's a dragon!

came from its mouth.

Thomas raised his head. He had dived to the ground at the dragon's approach and he was not alone there now. Everyone who was still in the market place was hugging paving stones tightly. They all watched in horror as the dragon stooped once again.

Close by stood a broad and ancient oak. For hundreds of years it had shaded old men from the noon sun. The dragon opened its jaws and dove upon the tree. In a heartbeat the tree's trunk became a tower of fire. People groaned in wonder and despair.

Like a great crow, the dragon settled on the roof of a counting house. The building was sturdy, stone and timber, but it sagged beneath the beast's weight. Roaring all the while, the dragon began smashing the house with great blows from its armored tail. Three such blows it struck and then it paused. Its red eyes stared out over the people sprawled on the stones beneath it.

It roared once again and flexed its corded muscles. Claws, steely hard, sank deep into roof timbers. With a surge of its mighty wings the dragon rose. Boards tore and beams snapped as a section of the counting house roof rose with it. The dragon lifted its burden smoothly into the sky and flew over the market place. People screamed and covered their heads. Thomas, Columbine and Pepper huddled against the fountain.

The dragon flew high over the harbor. It circled once and then dropped the tangle of boards and shingles it carried. The shattered roof fell into blue water with a tremendous splash. Everyone looked up to see what had happened. Thomas was about to suggest making a run for it when Pepper said, "Look!"

The dragon, gliding like a hawk, was coming back toward Silvershell. Lower and lower it came. Then, light as dandelion fluff, it landed on the stone quay beside a fishing boat. An uneasy stillness settled over the town and its people. The dragon sat statue-still on the quay. Gray smoke came from its nostrils. Some people rose to their feet to better see what the beast was doing. The dragon waited.

More and more people rose to their feet, Thomas among them. The dragon still did not move.

Columbine brushed her skirt and said, "Well, the beastie has had its fun. Now it wants something from us, I'll wager."

Pepper nodded and Thomas said nothing. There were frightened stirrings in the crowd. After several moments, Thomas saw movement at the far side of the market place. Six men were walking toward the quay. They were the mayor, the sheriff, and four deputies. They had seen their duty and were bravely, if reluctantly, approaching the dragon. Step by cautious step, they walked out upon the quay. Only smoke above the dragon's head moved, floated heavily on light morning airs. Some thirty feet from the monster's softly shining teeth, they stopped.

The mayor breathed deeply and took one more step forward. For once in his life he did not want to say a word. But he knew that he had to speak and cleverly so. He said, "We . . . we of Silvershell . . . ah, welcome you, oh mighty dragon."

The dragon looked mildly at the mayor. It opened its mouth and spoke, "I accept your welcome . . . for what it's worth." The voice was smooth and deep, not at all the sort of voice Thomas had expected to hear.

The mayor continued, "We . . . we are, of course, not accustomed to having such great, great visitors as yourself. We . . . we would like to give you a gift . . . ."

The dragon said, "I see. I suppose that in return for this gift you would expect me to . . . behave myself?"

The mayor smiled tentatively and said, "Your most awesome arrival did do some small damage to our town. Also, I'm sure, some people were surprised and alarmed at your coming." The mayor finished with a bow, his deepest and most official looking bow.

The dragon looked at them and remained silent for a long moment. The sheriff and his men twisted their fingers nervously beneath its red gaze. Finally, it said, "Very well. Very well. And . . . what is this soothing gift which you wish to bestow upon me?"

The mayor took a small, eager step forward, "Legend has it that members of your noble and ancient tribe have great love for beautiful things, things of gold and silver. We wish to give you our town's chest of treasure."

The dragon was silent.

The mayor waved his hands frantically, "And . . . and . . . and four large jars of pearls collected over many years by our island's fishermen!"

The dragon's eyes flashed scarlet with wrath. It opened its mouth and roared, "Fools!" A river of flame washed over the mayor, the sheriff, and the deputies. They jumped for their lives and tumbled headlong into the harbor's cold water. Splashing and blowing, they rose to the surface. The gold threads in the mayor's vest were melted and the sheriff's moustache was singed. Otherwise, they were all safe. Fearfully, they began to swim for shore.

The dragon ranted behind them, pounding its tail against the stones of the quay. "Fools! Fools! I am a tiger of the sun. You offer me kitten's milk. Fools! I am death! I am destruction! I have come from the wastes of time to teach you of fire and of the darkness after it. You hope to bribe me? With a teacupful of gold? Fools!"

The people of Silvershell shrank back and covered their eyes. Thomas expected the dragon to rise up in fire and destroy the town. Indeed few people there could have thought differently.

At that moment an old woman stepped onto the quay. She was thin and tiny, and her hair shone silver-

The dragon's eyes flashed scarlet with wrath.

bright in the sun. She walked with slow, firm steps toward the dragon.

Pepper whispered, "That is Mere Rowan. The mayor is as you have seen him. Mere Rowan is the wise one of our town. The dragon will listen to her, or to no one."

Mere Rowan now stood near dragon claws. She was bent with age, but not with fear. Instantly the dragon became quiet. The small woman stared into the eyes of the monster. It quickly looked down. Everyone watched in wonder.

The dragon spoke at last with a voice of honey and oil, "Ah, mother. You've come to speak with me. Only the dignity of your age can begin to know the dignity and vast purpose of mine."

Mere Rowan smiled coldly, "I know."

The dragon went on, "I have slept a hundred hundred voyages of the moon. Only this day have I awakened."

Mere Rowan said, "You have awakened and brought us sorrow. And greater sorrow is to come, I guess. Dragon, what do you want? We are at your small mercy."

The dragon rose up on its legs and spread its wings wide. Mere Rowan did not move. It spoke and its voice was now like an iron bell, "I come for what is my due. I come for all the gold in this island, every grain. I come for every polished jewel, every piece of silver. I come for every lamb, every cow. I come for every sack of grain, every basket of fruit, every barrel of wine. I have slept long. My hunger is great."

The old woman said nothing. What could she say?

The dragon went on, "I am going to leave. On the

third day from this, at noon, I shall return. All of your wealth, all of your food must be gathered here by then. If even a little is kept from me, my anger will burn your island black."

There was silence. The dragon stared past Mere Rowan at the people of the town. Its eyes were cold now, green as ice. Thomas looked into them and saw an endless winter night.

Mere Rowan backed away from the dragon. It glanced down at her and spoke again, "Three days. I return in three days." Then it leapt into the sky. In fire and thunder it flew out over the sea.

EVENING

The old man leaned back in his chair. He was silent for long moments. The children looked at him expectantly, but he said nothing. They then turned and watched small blue flames in the fire and also said nothing, for they were beginning to know the moods of their story-teller. At last the old man rose to his feet and said, "It's time for us to fix supper."

The boy and the girl rose to help him. Storm claws of wind and rain raked at the cabin, but the children paid them no heed. Their minds were busy with dragons, with ways of defeating dragons. They spoke hardly at all while they helped to lentil soup and cut pieces of bread.

With supper over and dishes cleared away, the old man went back to his carving. The boy and the girl played castles and clowns, a popular game in their town. Their laughter, loud at first, slowly stilled. Night was coming. Storm-bear again breathed coldly on them.

The old man rose from his work. He muttered and dropped his knife on the desk. He walked to the wide sink. He pulled at the pump handle several times and drew himself a cup of cold water. He drank it noisily. The children smiled behind their hands. He walked stiffly to his chair and sat down. He said, "Well, you're probably wondering how Mere Rowan is going to deal with that dragon. Eh?" The children nodded and looked into his bright, deep eyes.

The children looked into his bright deep eyes.

THE LEMON TREE

Thomas was hungry. Much had happened since the dragon's departure, but not supper. He and Pepper and Columbine had helped others to clear away broken boards and shattered stones. Some people, too, had been hurt and had needed doctoring. The mayor, fortified by brandy and by his best silk waistcoat, had appeared and called a town meeting. Then all of the people who were not busy with the wounded had filed into the town hall.

Thomas looked around the shadowy hall and wondered what would happen next. He lowered his eyes as Pepper began to speak to the disturbed gathering, "We must fight! We must fight! We can't let this dragon rob us of everything we own!" Silence closed darkly around his words. Thomas heard a nervous shuffling of feet against stone.

Finally, a fat grocer spoke, "Fight with what? We have no weapons beyond an odd sword or two. We certainly have no time to make new ones. Besides, what weapon do we know of that could possibly hurt, much less kill a dragon?"

The miller's son blurted out, "A stone! We could drop a huge stone on it."

"Rubbish!" said the burly blacksmith. "Can you imagine it? Here, handsome dragon, come over here. Come over to this mountain so we can drop a nice stone on your head. Hold still . . . rubbish!"

The miller stood up and shook his fist, "Take that back, Smith. You can't make my son out to be a fool!"

The blacksmith grinned, "I've no need to do that. People know he's a fool just by looking at his father."

There was a roar of laughter. The miller howled and jumped from his seat. There would have been a terrible fight if the sheriff's deputies, somewhat recovered from their morning's swim, had not come between the two men.

The mayor pounded his gavel on the table in front of him, "Hold! Hold! Listen to me! Listen!" The crowd quieted and he continued, "Certainly it must be obvious to you what we should do. Our only hope is to do exactly what the dragon wants. We have no other choice. We can't fight the beast without weapons. Let us begin now to gather our wealth."

Pepper jumped to his feet and shouted, "No! Fight!"

The grocer shouted, "Hear the mayor! Give the dragon gold and food. It will kill us all if we don't!"

Shouts of "Yes!" and "No!" were coming from all sides. The meeting was quickly becoming one great and furious argument. Then Mere Rowan walked toward the front of the hall. She reached the mayor, turned, and stood facing the noisy crowd. She waited. Elbows were jostled into ribs and quickly everyone became silent.

She slowly turned her head, looking into the eyes of each person there. At last she spoke, "We share great peril. To fight this dragon is impossible. It is strong and evil beyond our understanding. To buy it off, to bribe it, is also impossible."

The mayor said, "But why? Why shouldn't it leave us alone after it has taken all of our wealth?"

Mere Rowan smiled coldly, "The greed of dragons is a matter of legend. Be assured, this dragon wants both our wealth and our lives. It hopes that we will gather our treasure and food into one place. Then it can burn and kill as it wishes without fear of destroying anything it might want later." Mere Rowan again looked over the faces of the towns- people. She waited for the meaning of her words to sink in. A cold snow of fear fell on the hearts of everyone there as they understood.

The mayor said, "But . . . but what are we to do?"

Pepper quickly said, "Mere Rowan, you would not speak to us in this way if you had no hope. Do you know of some spell, some magic that might save us?"

Mere Rowan's eyes were bright, "Pepper, you know me better than that. I do not deal in dead frogs and darkness. My magic is of gardens growing, of flowing waters." She paused and smiled, "However, there is something . . . something. I will leave tonight in search of it. I will climb over the top of Snowmane and try to prove the truth of old stories."

People glanced nervously at each other. Some argued softly about what Mere Rowan had just said. Thomas whispered, "What is Snowmane?"

Pepper said, "Snowmane is the highest mountain in our island, and the farthest east. Unclimbable cliffs rise from the sea to guard all its approaches. Its summit is wrapped in deep snows and even deeper stories. No one has ever climbed it or seen its far side. Some have tried, but none who have gone high on the mountain have ever returned."

Mere Rowan held up her hand. Everyone became quiet once again. She said, "I go into danger. I will need help. Is there one among you who will go with me?"

Many heads turned toward the blacksmith. He was seated on a stool at the back of the hall. He rose to his feet. His calm eyes rested on Mere Rowan, "Yes, Lady, I am strong, as strong as I ever was. But my beard is too gray, my legs too stiff. I move too slowly. I would be of no help to you. Twenty years ago . . . but not now. How about the miller's lad? He's as strong as I am and he's as swift as a deer, if his boasts can be believed."

Heads turned again. The miller's boy stood near the western wall. His thick-muscled arms hung down at his sides. He had long been the strongest boy in town. He had also long been the town's worst bully. Now it seemed that people expected him to do something truly brave. His face went white with fear. Desperately, he looked from side to side. His wide, round eyes came to rest on Thomas. "The giant," he cried, "the giant should go! He's far stronger than I."

Thomas took a deep breath. Everyone was now looking at him. Suddenly, he knew what he should do. For all of his life he had lived on the farthest edges, in the deepest shadows. A number of accidents had now pushed him into the center, into strong light. In a clear voice, which he scarcely recognized as his own, he said, "Yes! I will go with you, Mere Rowan, and gladly so."

Mere Rowan smiled warmly, "Well said, my boy! I accept your offer of help. We will leave as soon as I can gather my belongings. Meet me at the fountain in an hour's time." She turned to the mayor. "Now you, all of you," she motioned to the people of the town, "you must not be idle while we are gone. Gather the treasure. Gather the food. Take it all to the market place. It will fool the dragon into thinking that we are doing what it wishes us to do. If I come back, we will have a chance of saving all. If I don't come back . . . fight for your lives as best you can." She turned and walked toward the door.

Loud talking broke out everywhere. Columbine took one of Thomas's arms and Pepper took the other. They led him quickly outside. Pepper said, "That was a brave thing you did in there. You don't know how brave, I think. Snowmane will teach you that."

Columbine said, "Hush, my husband. We have work to do. Young Thomas will freeze long before he gets anywhere near the top of Snowmane if we don't find proper clothes for him. Come, my cousin Ned lives around this corner. He can help us." They walked briskly into the dusk.

An hour later Thomas was standing beside the fountain. He wore soft leather leggings and a leather vest. Under his arm was a thick robe of fur which had originally been made for someone's bed. On his head he wore a fur cap. Ned had been helpful indeed. He had worked miracles with scissors and leather thongs.

Also, Columbine had found fresh bread and a pot of honey in her cousin's pantry. Thomas had been able to nicely cure his hunger with these and several glasses of cold milk. Now he felt quite ready and able to fight the dragon by himself.

Pepper said, "Here comes Mere Rowan."

Columbine smiled at the old woman and said, "We've fixed him up as well as we could at such short notice."

Mere Rowan said, "I'm sure you have, Columbine." She turned to Thomas. "Well, my boy, we must be off. Are you ready?"

Thomas nodded. At that moment both Pepper and Columbine reached up and hugged him. He was a little embarrassed, but very pleased. He felt, in truth, so full of warmth that he was sure that no mountain could chill him.

Mere Rowan untied the reins of a gray pony. Slowly, gracefully, she mounted it. She said, "Here, Thomas. You lead the black pony. It will carry what food we need and more warm clothing."

Thomas came forward and took the black pony's lead rope. Mere Rowan waved at Pepper and Columbine. She clucked to her pony and it began walking away from the fountain. Thomas waved to his two friends and saw their hands rise in reply. He said nothing, but quickly followed after Mere Rowan.

They walked through torch-lit streets. Now and then someone would wave to them, but most were too busy. Much had to be done in order to prepare for the dragon's second visit.

The old woman and the boy soon passed beneath Silvershell's eastern gate. They followed a winding road which climbed steadily into wooded hills. Thomas was excited. Darkness covered the hills with mystery. There were many things to look at. He had to be wary, though, for the black pony, not happy with this night journey, often tried to nip him.

Night was old when Mere Rowan stopped. They were in a broad, grassy meadow. She slid slowly from her pony's back and said, "I'm tired, Thomas, and so must you be. Let's rest here until dawn."

Thomas said, "I could keep going."

"No," said Mere Rowan quietly, "great tests await us. We'll need our strength for the mountain. Let's rest now."

Then the old woman hobbled the ponies so that they could graze. Thomas fetched water from a stream nearby. Soon they were both lying on the grass wrapped in their cloaks. Mere Rowan suddenly snored quite loudly. Thomas judged that she was asleep. He was too excited to sleep. Instead he watched the stars. They swung in great silver arcs across the sky.

He blinked his eyes. The stars had disappeared. He blinked again and shook his head. He had slept after all. The sun was just nosing its way above a line of young fir trees.

Mere Rowan was saddling the gray pony. She turned when she heard him rise, "Good morning, Thomas. Let's be off. We must be high on Snowmane's shoulder before the sun sets today." Thomas nodded and hurriedly rolled up his cloak.

They began walking. The road became a path and grew steeper. Hills became mountains as the morning passed.

At noon they came to a vast canyon. It was narrow, but its sides plunged a thousand feet to a rocky valley far below. Thomas gulped. A slender arch of stone was the only path to the far side. Mere Rowan did not slow down at all. She guided her pony almost carelessly out onto the bridge. Thomas swallowed hard again and followed. He kept his eyes straight ahead and reached the other side without incident. Mere Rowan's eyes sparkled with amusement as she watched him step carefully onto solid ground. The black pony clopped lazily after him. She said, "Thomas, we'll stop for a rest soon. We should eat something."

Thomas said, "Please, I'm hungry."

A few moments later, they came to a group of large boulders. At its base they found a deep pool of water. The ponies headed for it with no urging. Mere Rowan dismounted and removed a small package from her saddlebag. Thomas knelt at the pool's edge and drank. The water was very cold and had a soft, snowmelt taste.

Mere Rowan seated herself in a shady spot and offered him a brown cake. Thomas thanked her and took a bite. It was crumbly and sweet with honey. He quickly finished the one he had and took another.

Mere Rowan idly brushed a crumb off her dress and said, "We should push on quickly, but I'll take some time now to explain to you just what we are about, what we hope to find. It's important that you know. I can speak freely now that we're far from the town. Are you curious?"

Thomas nodded. He had no idea what they could find at the top of a mountain which would help them to defeat the dragon. He had wondered, but had not felt free to ask.

Mere Rowan went on, "Let me say first that this dragon is far stronger than anyone suspects. It is not just a rather large, ill-tempered lizard. No, it is a monster, an evil monster. Have you known evil in your life, Thomas?"

Thomas thought of the fisherman's bitter face, of the cold stone that his hunger became when he'd had nothing to eat for a day. He looked at Mere Rowan and said, "Bad things have happened to me. And sometimes people have done bad things to me. I don't know if you could call them evil."

Mere Rowan thought for a moment and then said, "Evil is harm, Thomas. It is harm which need never have happened. It is harm caused willfully and it is harm caused by neglect. Have you known such harm?"

"Yes," said Thomas softly. "Yes."

"And good? You've known goodness, too?"

"Yes."

"So have we all. Good and evil, evil and good — they are twin forces, ever growing. They work through all of us, through our acts." Mere Rowan took a sip of water from a flask at her side.

Thomas thought for a moment and then said, "What has this to do with the dragon?"

"Ah, Thomas," said Mere Rowan as she put down the flask of water, "indeed what should evil have to do with a dragon? It was only a beast once. Evil has turned it into a monster.

"People die, Thomas, but the spirit of their deeds lives on in the world. And so the spirit of evil deeds slowly regathers and takes form — within the dragon. For long years this dragon has lain asleep on flinty stones. Murder, war, treacheries of all kinds, starvation — all the currents of past dark deeds have flowed to it, over it. It has soaked in the acid hatreds of a thousand years. Its fires have been fueled by uncounted sufferings.

"When it was at last full to bursting with evil, it awoke. It is strong now with an unnatural power. It must no longer lie quietly among stones. And it is hungry. It hungers to release the evil power it contains, spew it forth, once again, onto the world. There will be death, red fire in the night. Silvershell is only the first town it will destroy."

Thomas shook his head, "Then why are we making this journey? What can we find on the mountain which will stop this dragon?"

Mere Rowan looked at him, her eyes clear and gray.

60

At last she said, "I have lived long, Thomas, and have learned much. Yet, I know only the smallest part of what there is to know. One thing I have found to be true is that there is balance in this world. Balance — a word which gives me hope. There are forces, too, for great good. They do exist. They do.

"It is true that the forces of evil, like this dragon, cut a jagged path across the sky. The music of thunder and drums sounds loudly for them. Fear falls like rain from their smokey clouds of war. But . . . there are forces of good which can counter them.

"One such force is what we now seek. Old stories say that it may be found on the southern flank of Snowmane."

"What is it?" Thomas asked.

"A tree," replied Mere Rowan. "A tree from the world's beginning. This tree takes in our world's goodness just as the dragon has gathered its evil. The spirits of kindness, of gifts given, of sacrifices willingly made for others are carried to Snowmane by clean, cold winds. The tree bathes in these airs and warm sunshine falls upon it. It produces a fruit of wondrous sweetness. And there is a power in the fruit's sweetness, a power for good which, so stories say, will wash away evil's bitterest acid."

Thomas asked, "What kind of tree is it?"

"It is a lemon tree. We must find it and take one of

its lemons. Then, with a little luck, we can defeat the dragon."

Thomas looked doubtfully at Mere Rowan and said, "How can a lemon defeat a dragon? That's ridiculous."

"My boy, think a bit. This dragon is invulnerable to all the weapons of evil — swords, fire, bombs, blades of every kind. No such weapon will bite upon it. It has been made strong through evil deeds accomplished by the use of such weapons. It is well armored against them. But kindness? Gentleness? Love? These are poison to such a beast. The fruit we seek is a distillation of all good things. Should the dragon eat it, its powers of destruction and death would be beaten down by the lemon's power of life. It would become a statue, frozen by goodness for thousands of years."

"But how," said Thomas, "will we get the dragon to eat the lemon? It's not stupid."

"No," said Mere Rowan, "it's not stupid, but it is proud. It is very proud. Its pride can be used against it. Be patient. I am giving the matter thought. Besides, you've forgotten that we do not yet have the magical lemon. First things first!"

Thomas thought for a moment and then said, "The dragon will not die from eating the lemon?"

"No, it won't."

"Then it will come back someday. What will

happen?"

Mere Rowan sighed, "Someone will have to find a different way to subdue it. I know of no final victories, my boy. But one can hope that at the end of all things evil will be gone and that a little good will still be left."

She cupped her hands, filled them with cold water and splashed her face with it. Thomas looked out across rocky hills and then down at his own arm, warm in the sun.

Mere Rowan said, "Ah, that's better. Come, Thomas. Our deed is not yet done, far from it!" She rose and walked to her pony. Thomas took up the black's lead rope again. They set out.

Hours passed as the path led them higher and higher. Granite peaks fell away beneath and behind them. Thomas, during a brief rest, looked down with wonder on the tops of clouds. At dusk they came to a field of snow.

Mere Rowan said, "The ponies can go no farther. Our climb begins here. I must now walk with you." She looked at the sky. "Let's rest and have something to eat. We will have to wait anyway until the moon rises."

Two hours later, Thomas looked up at a sea of silver. The moon had just risen and touched the snowfield with magic light. He glanced down at the black metal spikes on his feet and then back at Mere Rowan. "Are you sure that these things will work?" he asked.

She laughed and said, "You would slide straight back to Silvershell if you didn't wear them. Believe me!"

Thomas again looked doubtfully at the sets of iron spikes strapped to his feet. Mere Rowan continued, "Night has made the snow hard and slippery, but safer too. It won't fall to the sea beneath us."

Thomas nodded and then carefully walked out onto the snow. His spikes bit deeply with each step and made a solid crunching sound. It took him only a few steps to gain confidence in his strange footgear. Then he began to enjoy himself. Mere Rowan labored heavily behind him.

An hour of steady plodding passed. Thomas kept his eyes on the snow before him and worked his way upwards. He halted at the base of a black cliff. It stood tall and smooth in front of him. He wondered how they were to climb it.

Mere Rowan shouted from far below, "Thomas! Thomas! Come back, Thomas!"

He turned in surprise. He had thought that she was right behind him. He shaded his eyes from the moon's glare off the snow and saw her. Leaping and sliding, he plunged back down the slick slope toward her.

Mere Rowan was sitting wearily in the snow. She looked up as he approached and said, "Ah, Thomas, you will have to go on alone. This is too hard for me. I had feared as much." She coughed dryly.

Thomas said, "We can rest for a bit. I'll help you then. We can make it together."

"No, my boy. I'm tired, too tired to continue. There is no path to the top for me. Go on. Find the tree. Bring back one lemon. And hurry! There is so little time."

Thomas said, "But what about you? I can't leave you!"

The old woman smiled, "Don't worry. I shall rest here for awhile. Then I should be able to make my way back down to the ponies. I will meet you there. Now, go. Go, and my blessing go with you." She reached for his hand and held it tightly for a brief moment.

Thomas grinned and said, "I'll be back soon and I'll have a lemon with me!" He turned and set off across the high reaches of the snow field.

He stopped again at the foot of the great crag. He looked to his right and saw that it continued unbroken into darkness. He looked to his left. A ribbon of snow led up the face of the cliff and disappeared around its far edge. He walked to his left.

He found that the white ribbon was a thin ledge of rock covered by several inches of snow. At no place was it wider than three feet. In many places it was far narrower than that. Thomas swallowed hard. It was the only way. He had to take it.

Step after careful step, he worked his way upwards. He soon rounded the cliff's edge and climbed slowly up the side of Snowmane's great head. Two miles and more below his left hand was the sea.

He came to a section where black rock showed through the white crust. He hesitated and then stepped onto it. Suddenly, his feet flew out from under him. Even as he fell, he realized that the rock was covered with hard, clear ice. He landed on his stomach with a stunning crash. His legs slid over the edge of the cliff. He flung his arms wide. His left arm scraped over knife edges of rock. His right hit a stone knob which was free of ice. His fingers clutched at it, clutched and held.

Thomas gasped, tried to force air into his bruised chest. He glanced over his shoulder and found that he was hanging by his finger-tips above the sea. His fingers slipped a tiny fraction of an inch. He squeezed the rock harder and felt his muscles twist into painful knots. Fear grinned at him with a dragon's gaping mouth, pulled at him from the sea's black deeps.

He thought of Mere Rowan, of how she had held his hand only a short time before. He thought of the lemon tree, of its promise. He thought of Pepper and Columbine, of their kindness to him. He thought of dragonfire.

Then, shuddering once, he pushed fear from his mind and fought to live. His feet scraped over icy rock. The spikes on his right foot caught on a tiny ledge. He stood on it and it held. His left foot found a narrow crack. Slowly, painfully, he pulled himself out of dark air and back onto the path.

He finally lay with his face against ice. Pain and cold were at war within his body. Blood dripped onto the snow from his torn arm. A thin voice in his mind cried out for rest, for sleep. Then Mere Rowan came before his mind's eye and he knew that he must not wait, must not rest. He had to go on. He had to keep his promise.

He sat up. With strips torn from his shirt he bandaged his arm. The wound was a bad one, a deep and ragged tear, but he could do nothing more for it. He shakily got to his feet. Keeping his right hand against the mountain, he once more began to labor up the icy ledge.

He climbed. His arm throbbed redly. A cutting wind blew down from the stars. Hours passed, hours of cold, hours of pain. But he had to reach the mountain's peak. He had to push on past it and find the magic lemon tree. He climbed.

Dawn at last washed over Thomas in a gentle flood of pearl-silver light. He blinked his eyes tiredly. He had not even noticed its coming. He looked up. Only a small hill of snow was above him. He had done it. He was nearly at Snowmane's highest point.

He thrashed forward as quickly as he could. He made his way over the rounded summit and started down the mountain's far side. The new day grew wide around him as he slipped and slid down a gentle snowfield. At the end of the snowfield was the verge of a great cliff. It fell in a steep cascade of stone down, down to the breaking waves. Thomas saw these things through a smokey haze of pain.

Then the sun rose and its swords of light cut through the mists in his mind. The bright light revealed to him what he had come to find. Gold-crowned by dawn, the lemon tree stood in a sun-warm alcove. Its leaves were dark green, its branches heavy with fruit.

Thomas stumbled up to it and sat down heavily beside its trunk. A sweet, wonderful smell filled the still air around him. He leaned against the tree. Warm sunlight fell on his shoulder. He smiled and instantly fell asleep. The branches of the tree spread protectively above him.

SECOND NIGHT

The old man rose to his feet and stretched. The children looked at him and then nervously glanced at the cabin's walls. The thick logs were groaning under the pressure of the wind.

The old man said, "Our fire needs wood. I'll get some from the box. You two stay put." Fear shone in the children's eyes. They didn't move.

The old man walked to the wood box, bent down, and began loading pieces of wood onto his left arm. After a moment, he stood up. He looked out of the window. Worry deepened the lines in his face. The storm was trying one last time to kill them.

He turned and said, "Well, it should be time for bed. I suppose, though, that there's no getting to sleep with all of this sorry noise going on. So, I'll finish my story." He walked to the fire, dropped a log on it, and put the rest of the wood on the brick hearth. He sat down.

The children moved closer to the orange flames and, at the same time, closer to the old man's slippered feet. The old man smiled, reached out and gently mussed the boy's hair. He said, "There's evil in storms as well as dragons, no?"

The children nodded.

"But don't worry. My walls are thick; my roof, stout." He nodded, almost to himself, and then continued, "Now, do you see what has happened to Thomas?"

The children looked at each other and then back at the old man. Their minds turned away from fear to consider his question. The boy said, "What do you mean?"

"Confidence," answered the old man, "confidence. He has it now. Don't you see what a difference it makes?"

The girl, firelight making orange stars in her eyes, thought for a moment before answering, "No. No, I don't think so."

The old man looked at her intently.

She went on, "I think he's forgotten to be afraid. He's forgotten about himself, about his problems."

"Yes," said the boy, "he's too worried about Mere Rowan, and Pepper, and Columbine to be afraid."

The old man looked from one to the other. Another smile, a slight curve only, passed like a cloud's shadow over his lips. He said, "We must speak further of this. But now, where was I?"

The boy said, "At the lemon tree."

"Yes, the lemon tree. And then . . . the dragon."

DRAGONFEAST

Thomas awoke with a start. Morning was nearly gone. For a moment he was confused. Then he looked up and saw green branches, the lemon tree.

Slowly he got to his feet and found that the power of the tree had worked its good upon him. His arm was sore, but not dreadfully so. His head was clear and he felt well rested.

He remembered his mission and looked again at the tree. His eye was drawn to a large, bright yellow lemon. Gently, careful not to bruise a leaf or bend a branch, he reached for it. It fell lightly into his hand just as his fingers touched it. Holding the lemon firmly, he backed away from the tree.

Thomas raised his eyes to the mist-blue sky. He knew that he should quickly begin his long journey back over and down the mountain, but a strange feeling now came over him. He did not want to leave. Warm air pushed softly at his face. Snow diamonds above the alcove broke sunlight into unnumbered rainbows. Far away, over a wave-jewelled sea, clouds sailed in white silence.

Thomas sighed. He knew in his heart that he would never again stand in a place so beautiful as this, or so dearly won. He felt at peace with himself and with the mountain. For the first time in his life he was alone, but not lonely. Once again, he looked at the wonderful tree. Its leaves moved slowly in a graceful dance with sun and wind.

He turned and began walking. He did not look back. A sadness which he could not explain filled his eyes with tears.

Soon, though, he had to pay attention to where his feet were taking him. He crossed over the snowy summit and again came to the narrow ledge where he had fallen. He carefully tested each foothold as he made his way down. He used his left hand to grasp knobs on the mountain's wall while in his right he carried the sun-yellow fruit.

Snowmane was kind to him on that downward journey. The ice was gone, but the snow was still firm. An hour after passing the difficult place, he reached Mere Rowan and the ponies.

She got stiffly to her feet when she saw him coming. There was great happiness in her smile, in her eyes. Strangely, Thomas did not feel able to talk as he came up to her. She understood this and also said nothing. She helped him sit down on a warm rock. She took the lemon and put it in her saddlebag. She then washed his wounds in snowmelt water and wrapped them with clean bandages.

Finally, Thomas looked up and said, "I'm thirsty! And hungry!"

Mere Rowan laughed and said, "You should be, Thomas, you should be. You've done something which no other person in this island has ever done. I'll bring you honey-cakes and water. I have nothing better to offer you now. Later, if the dragon is defeated, I shall fix you a supper such as you have never had before. I promise!"

Thomas smiled and said, "I guess that we should start back to Silvershell."

"Yes," said Mere Rowan, "we have less than a day. It's a race now, Thomas, and we must be the swiftest. But first you shall eat and drink." Mere Rowan brought him the cakes and her flask of water. He drank deeply. He then ate the cakes and drank again. Before many minutes had passed, they began their journey back to Silvershell.

Thomas did not see the mountains or the hours through which they passed. Mists veiled his eyes, mists of pain and tiredness. Rough stones hurt his feet. Dust scratched his eyes. His arm began to throb again. The ponies plodded heavily on.

At dusk they passed over the narrow bridge which had so frightened him before. This time he scarcely noticed it. He had, after all, been in much higher places since his first crossing.

Night folded itself around them. They traveled on. Mere Rowan swayed wearily in her saddle. Thomas stumbled on, tired beyond measure. Sleep would have been the richest of all treasures to them both, but they had no time for sleeping. The dragon was coming. Each time his eyes threatened to close, Thomas remembered its terrible face.

Dawn found them on the hills above Silvershell. Seeing the town in the distance below helped them a great deal. They found new strength and began to descend.

They walked through Silvershell's eastern gate at midmorning. A crowd of very nervous people awaited them and some even started to cheer. Others quickly quieted the noisy ones. The dragon was due to arrive soon. It would be most suspicious if it saw a celebration taking place.

The mayor came up and spoke a few quiet words with Mere Rowan. Columbine and Pepper pushed their way through the crowd and came to Thomas's side.

Pepper shouted, "Welcome home, Thomas! We feared we'd never see you again!"

Columbine spoke more quietly, "Look at your arm! What have you been up to? Come with me and let me care for that."

Thomas laughed and said, "I think I'd better wait. Mere Rowan may need me to help her. I'll be fine."

Columbine looked doubtfully at his bandages, but nodded her consent. At that moment Mere Rowan said, "Thomas, we have only a few minutes. The dragon will soon be here. We must be ready for it." She started off toward the harbor.

Thomas patted Columbine's shoulder and said, "There'll be time for bandages and for visiting after the dragon is defeated. Wait for me." He smiled at his two friends and turned to follow Mere Rowan.

They walked through narrow streets. At last they came to the market place. Great changes had taken place there. Boxes, baskets, and large iron-bound chests were everywhere. The wealth of the island had indeed been assembled.

Mere Rowan turned to Thomas and said, "Now comes the hardest time. Pride — pride is the key. The dragon's pride must be challenged. I'm not sure what I will do. I'll have to improvise, but I'll begin by making it think that we have given up, that we are begging for its mercy. I will offer it a basket full of the finest fruits. Among them will be the magical lemon. And then . . . we'll see. The mayor is bringing the basket now. Will you come with me and carry it for me?"

Thomas swallowed and said, "Yes, I've come this far so I should help finish the job."

"Good!" said Mere Rowan. "Remember to act frightened. It will expect that of you."

Thomas grinned, "I won't have to act."

Mere Rowan glanced at the sky. "I'll flatter the beast and . . . " her words drifted into silence.

Thomas looked up. Far above he saw a speck in the sky. It quickly grew larger. He felt a tugging at his arm.

He turned and looked down into the mayor's worried eyes. The small man said nothing, but handed him a basket piled high with fruit. Mere Rowan reached over and placed the lemon on the very top of the pile. The mayor swiftly backed away.

Thomas looked up again. He could see the dragon's wings beating with the slow, patient power of ocean waves. Behind him a few people peeked out around the edges of boxes and bales. Most, though, were hidden in cellars or deep places in the forest. The dragon was close now. It circled the market place one time and gently glided to a landing on the quay.

Mere Rowan said, "Well, Thomas, it's time." With small, hesitant steps she began to approach the dragon. Thomas followed her, carrying the heavy basket.

The dragon watched them, its eyes as mild and green as a summer sea. It said nothing. Thomas became increasingly uneasy under that unblinking stare.

At last they stood close to it, just beneath its heavy jaws. Thomas could feel his heart trying to break loose from within his chest and hide somewhere around his toes. The dragon seemed far larger close up than when it had been in the air. Its scales shone with many colors. Its claws were steely blue. Its black tongue curled around ivory teeth. Thomas dared not look into its eyes.

Mere Rowan said, "Welcome, oh Lord of the Skies. We have done your bidding." She bowed.

The dragon watched her for long, silent moments. Finally, it said, "I had expected more from you, Mother. I had expected that you would not give in so easily. It is sensible of you, but somehow disappointing. The wise are less wise than they once were, it seems."

Mere Rowan said, "Where in the world can we find power to match yours, oh Mighty One? We can only surrender ourselves to your mercy."

The dragon rumbled softly with laughter, "My mercy? My mercy? I promised you nothing, Mother. Nothing."

Mere Rowan looked up at the dragon. She saw a yellow flame in its eyes. With great care she said, "We know. We hope only that the completeness, the richness of our gift to you will temper your anger."

She motioned to Thomas. He stepped in front of her and placed the basket on the ground. She produced a cloth of red velvet and spread it over the smooth stones. Her darting hands quickly transferred the fruit from the basket to the cloth. Near the very center she put the magic lemon. She straightened up and said, "Here is a sweet beginning for the long feast we have prepared for you. Taste, and enjoy!"

The dragon was silent for several more moments. Sunlight, reflected from the harbor's waters, danced in its eyes. It said at last, "Ah, Mother, perhaps I was wrong. You have not given up." Its voice was oily smooth, but its eyes had gone flame red.

Mere Rowan did not move. Thomas wanted to run for his life, but he knew that his first step would bring an ocean of flames.

The dragon went on, "Poison? You hope to poison me?" It opened wide its mouth and laughed. All the buildings of the town shook as if the earth had become jelly. Thomas fell to his knees. Mere Rowan stood still, sturdy as a tree stump.

The dragon, its voice again smooth, said, "Poison? Mother, my blood is the fiercest poison of all. I am proof against all lesser potions. And know this, Mother, know that my wrath will be more cunning, more terrible, if you have tried in some feeble way to harm me."

Mere Rowan looked steadily into the dragon's red eyes and said, "We have only brought you the finest fruits of our island. They are full of the goodness of sun and soil. They contain no poison." She reached down and picked up the lemon. Quickly she peeled it. She took one of its sections and put it in her mouth. She took another and gave it to Thomas. She said, "Eat it, Thomas."

He raised the fruit to his lips and bit into it. His eyes opened wide with surprise. He had never before tasted anything so good. It was not heavy and bitter like the lemons he had known, but light and sweet and bursting with juice.

The dragon watched them, its eyes narrow slits. Mere Rowan turned to it and held out the remainder of

You tricked me!

the lemon. It said, "So, I am challenged. I accept. Though I don't trust you, Mother. Something is not right about this. If you have tried to trick me, you will not go unpunished. Your death will be the last and longest of all."

Mere Rowan permitted herself a small smile.

With a snort of impatience the dragon flicked out its long tongue. It took the lemon from Mere Rowan's hand and swallowed it swiftly. Thomas wondered what would happen next. He was still wondering when Mere Rowan pulled him roughly to the ground.

The dragon bellowed with rage. Understanding and something that could have been fear came to its eyes. In a choking voice it said, "One of the first trees . . . that fruit . . . magic . . . you tricked me . . . Mother!"

Mere Rowan shouted, "No, dragon! Your pride tricked you. I have given you the best fruit of our island. Your evil chokes upon it!"

The dragon staggered. Green smoke frothed from its mouth. Suddenly, it made a mighty leap into the air. Its wings beat twice as it rose hundreds of feet above the town. Then it gave a strangled cry and fell. It crashed in ruin on a hill of sand beside the sea.

Thomas looked at Mere Rowan. Her eyes were shining with tears. Smiling, she took his hand and held it tightly.

STORM'S END — MORNING

The old man paused and listened. He could hear only faint whinings of wind. The storm was at last losing strength, dying. He glanced down at the children. They lay drowsily before the fire. The old man remained silent. In several moments the boy and the girl both slept.

The old man then rose, walked to the window and looked through dark air. He could dimly see stars. A smile passed quickly over his lips. He turned and went back to the children. He covered them with a thick quilt. They would sleep well on the soft hearth rug. In great weariness he walked to his bed.

The boy awoke to find sunshine streaming through the open cabin door. His sister was outside already. He rose and quickly joined her. Morning was warm and gentle around them. It was as if the storm had never happened.

The old man was sitting on a bench facing east. His knife was in his hand and he was whittling a stick. The children came over to him and sat down in the wet grass near his feet. Several quiet moments passed.

The boy, feeling a little uncomfortable, said, "That was a good story that you told us."

The old man said, "Thank you. I'm glad you liked it." Several more moments of silence passed.

Again, the boy spoke, "But . . . but what happened to the dragon? Was it dead? Did it just lie there?"

The old man grinned and said, "So, I'm not to escape without questions, eh?"

Both children smiled innocently at him.

"Well, all right. The dragon . . . the dragon. It did not die. It was, as Mere Rowan said, paralyzed by the power in the lemon from the first tree. It fell on the sand hill and lies there to this day. It can see and think, but it can do nothing else. The children of Silvershell play on it. Wonderful games can be invented around a real dragon. It will lie there for many years more. I suppose

It did not die.

that someday sands will drift over it, cover it again with a blanket of earth." The old man looked out across the sea.

The girl said, "What happened to the others — Thomas, Mere Rowan, Columbine and Pepper?"

The old man looked down at her, "Well, Mere Rowan went back to her animals and her garden. She lived many years more and was quite happy. She did, by the way, make Thomas the most delicious supper he had ever eaten, just as she had promised to do.

"Pepper and Columbine, of course, went back to their farm. They were prosperous and happy, though their work was hard.

"Thomas. . . . Now, Thomas stayed with Pepper and Columbine for a long while, and he was most helpful to them. He also was always welcome in Silvershell. He became great friends with the mayor and often played checkers with him."

The boy said, "But did he stay there? Did he live the rest of his life there, or did he get a boat and travel back to his own country?"

The old man laughed, "You've just asked me to tell you at least a dozen more stories. We haven't time for that! Have your mother bring you to me some other time. We can have lunch and I will spin yarns for you. Agreed?"

The children smiled and nodded their assent.

The old man stared at his carving for a moment and then said, "But now, you've asked many questions. I've answered them. Let me ask you one."

The children looked at him expectantly.

"Girl, what did you mean when you disagreed with me, when you spoke of caring?"

The girl blinked. She thought for a bit and then said, "About Thomas forgetting his own fear? About his worrying about Pepper, Columbine and Mere Rowan?"

"Yes," said the old man, "what exactly did you mean?"

"Well," she paused, "just that if you care about someone and that person is in trouble, you don't have time to worry about yourself. You do what must be done and you have no time to be afraid. That's not confidence, is it?"

The old man rubbed his chin, "No, you are right. It's not. I see now that I did not think clearly enough. Thomas did gain confidence from the difficult things he did, but the reason he did them was, as you said, his love for his friends. And I thought I was telling a story about confidence. It was really about caring and caring made him strong, not confidence. Good. Very good — the storyteller should always learn something from the telling of his story. Good!" He leaned forward and stretched his arms.

The girl watched the old man stretch. Her mouth

suddenly opened with surprise. From his left elbow to his left wrist ran a ragged scar, a very old scar, an ancient wound made perhaps by blades of icy rock. Her eyes met his. After a moment, he winked at her.

The boy scuffed his foot in the grass and said, "Well, I think that Thomas stayed there. He could walk around being a giant and have a great time. He would have been a fool to leave."

The old man laughed again and said, "He may not have been a fool, but he did leave. There was adventure in his leaving, too. Just wait. I'll tell you that story. Someday." He rose stiffly to his feet. "Now, I feel like a walk. Come with me, children. Let's see what the storm has brought to the cove."

They walked together down the long, steep path to the stony beach. Once there, they stood looking out over sparkling water. Small, sleepy waves lapped at their feet. A tide of sunshine flowed around them. Far away, deep in the blue swell of the sea, a white-sailed ship spread its wings before the morning breeze.

The End